1

God Loves Me!

Cellulite & All...

*Written
by
Jeri Darby
Ararity Press Publications*

*Special Thanks to
Illustrator*

Mayra Colao

God Loves Me...
Cellulite & All!
by
Jeri Darby

ISBN- 978-0-9979399-0-3   Ararity Press
ISBN- 0997939907

Ararity Press
Jeri Darby
P.O. Box 5682
Saginaw MI 48603

steppingstonesjd@gmail.com
989 717-1031

Dedication

This book is dedicated to every woman that

Struggles with weight issues

And...

has questioned

God's love.

To

Marilyn Zaball who showed me the path

to healthy weight loss...

To God, My Heavenly Father.

Jesus Christ, who is the Author and Finisher of my faith.

The Holy Spirit, my Comforter, Counselor, Guide and my

very best Friend...

Preface

Marilyn Zaball, a former co-worker overheard me mumbling to myself about the frustrations of my sudden weight gain. She invited me to a meeting- that very night and it was an answer to prayer! I attended and adopted the new practices and the weight melted! Before long I was fifty pounds lighter.

I thought I could improve on the wisdom that was freely given about food choices and discipline- *wrong!* Every lost pound found and stubbornly reattached itself to my body— plus some.

Weight is a serious issue; it impacts our health and self-esteem. When unhappy with our bodies it can hinder the growth and development needed to soar into our destinies. Even those who grasp the tools necessary to rid themselves of excess weight—cellulite is often the shocking aftermath and constant reminder.

Cellulite is the lumpy appearance beneath the skin especially in the hip and thighs. There is a myth that this only happens to overweight women— but men and thinner women can also have cellulite.

A healthy diet, routine exercise and massages are ways to decrease risk of cellulite. Hormonal balance and other factors can result in cellulite regardless. For many women and men... cellulite will be a lifelong reality. In a world that over emphasizes physical image it's important to remind ourselves that *true* beauty is visible to the heart rather than the limitations of the human eye.

Introduction

Mix a life *deficient* in exercise, *excessive* in sugar with years of working a desk job- you have a recipe for declining health, poor fitness and yes... cellulite. *"What happened to my body!"* I gawked. A full length mirror unveiled the aftermath of my life of inactivity. Though it seemed like it— these changes did *not* occur over night. I was too busy for too many years to notice the gradual changes. It was like I put on special glasses and began to see clearly. The reality was staggering!

"God Loves Me Cellulite and All..." is the title of the poem I wrote the same day; once I regained my composure. It inspired this book and is included within with illustrations. It deals with the emotional chaos that can follow changes in our body image. A lack of self-care, genetic predisposition and gradual weight gain over the years were among my causative factors. Many women battle emotional frustration and feelings of depression and helplessness when it comes to their bodies. This can trigger even more unhealthy eating habits.

"God yet loves me..." Grounding myself in this reality   appeased me for years as I dealt with the variation of my once slim frame. I am determined to upgrade my physical condition while reminding myself that there is *nothing* that could *ever* happen to my outer shell that would diminish God's love— for *me.* Nothing...

The Million Dollar Question

"Can you tell me how to rid my body
of cellulite caused by years of
inactivity- *overnight?*"
(Me…I asked my sister Lisa)

Answer…

"If you find out
Let me know and we
Will both be rich…"
Lisa

Table of Contents

God Loves

Me!

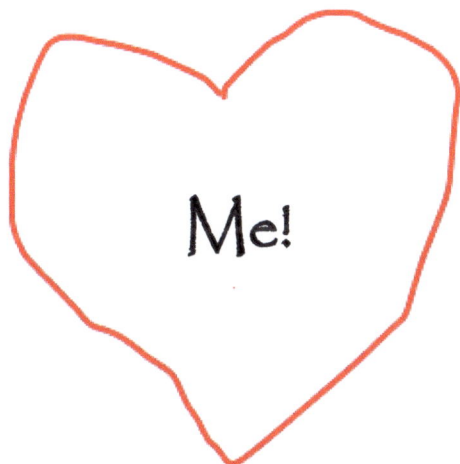

Cellulite & All...

God, I'm glad that
YOU LOVE
"ME,"
Cellulite and all.
I have to confess
that
SOMETIMES
I have felt
appalled.

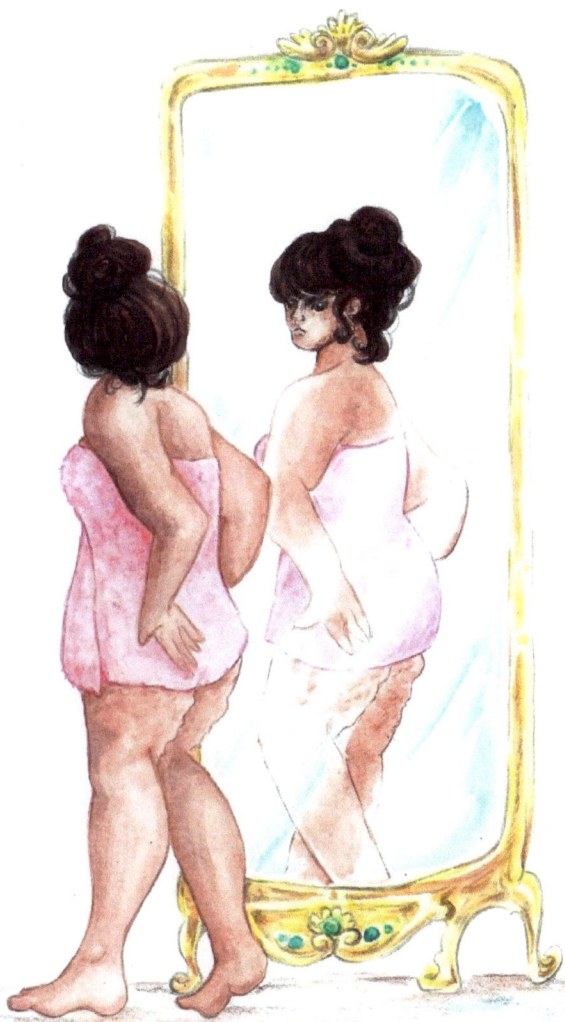

As

I

envision the

size; that

I

REALLY desire

to be,

Accomplishing
this task
SEEMS
IMPOSSIBLE
to ME.

I

try saying to

myself; OVER

and OVER again

I will just be a little

more disciplined!

Then this battle

I shall WIN!

Sometimes

I

lose a *few* pounds

And WOW!

Do I

feel GREAT!

Then...

With FOOD

I

began to

CELEBRATE!

THEN
BACK
COMES
the
WEIGHT!!!

Feeling
overly self-
conscious;
I fill with deep
REGRET
While thinking to
myself; "This is
NOT over yet!"

My God,
He LOVES me
dearly; regardless
of my size. The
beauty He
admires radiates
from INSIDE.

With
NEW
determination;
I'm SEEKING
to reach my goal.
It's such a burning
DESIRE
residing in my soul.

Such PEACE
I find in knowing;
a LOVE eternal,
profound
That shall be with
me *FOREVER*
whether my weight
is up or down.

A prayer...

Father, I am grateful to be your fearful and wonderfully made creation. I am thankful for the body you entrusted unto me. Forgive me for any neglect or mistreatment that I have put my body through over the years. I understand that not only is my body your temple; but it is the vehicle given me to fulfill your purpose in this world. Erase any negative emotions that I may harbor against the body that you have given me.

Open up the eyes of my understanding that I may adopt a healthy life plan that will work for my lifestyle. Lead and guide me to make the necessary changes that will restore my health, increase my endurance and improve my overall well-being.

Silence the condemning voice of satan that only bring feelings of rejection, self-loathing that results in doubts and fear on whether or not someone will love and accept me for me. Help me to walk in full assurance of your love. I am thankful to be part of your royal family.

Amen

About the Author

Jeri Darby is an author, speaker and songwriter who is committed to using the stepping stones in her life to soar into her destiny—while helping others along the way. She is all too familiar with the emotional aftermath following unwanted physical changes.

Jeri Darby is a registered nurse with over 25 years' experience working with those receiving mental health treatment. Jeri is passionate about equipping, encouraging and empowering women. She understands how a poor self-image can have a negative impact on every other area of our lives.

Jeri has ministered to men and women in jail, prison, halfway houses and shelters. She's served as president for both the Women's Weekend Retreat Outreach Ministry and Seeking and Waiting Singles Ministry which she was also founder and president. Jeri served 12 years as President of Aglow Int'l-Saginaw Lighthouse. Currently she is the director of the "The Father's Business" single's ministry at her local church and devoted to equipping, empowering and encouraging singles to tap into their God-given purpose and destiny while waiting on a marriage.

Jeri has ministered at conferences and written and directed plays addressing issues related to singles. She is a freelance writer and the story of how she began her nursing career has been published in 'Chicken Soup for the Nurse's Soul a Second Dose' (*Crisis Bridge*). There are over 100 publishing credits for her articles and poems appearing in Decision, Evangel, Women of Spirit, Upper Room, Women Alive!, Joyful Woman, Lookout, Standard, Righteous Nurse; Pentecostal Evangel, Purpose and others. She is currently writing Stepping Stones-Reflections for Singles Volume II.

Notes to Self

Thank you for purchasing

God Loves Me!
Cellulite and all...
Available in Spanish soon!

If you have enjoyed reading this
Watch for other illustrated poetry and books written
by
Jeri Darby

Other Publication
Stepping Stones
Daily Reflections for Singles - Volume I

Available Now on Amazon & Kindle
Barnes & Noble Online Market Place
Books a Million
Create Space E-Store

Stepping Stones – Reflections for Singles
Volume II
Soon to be released

www.ingramcontent.com/pod-product-compliance
Lightning Source LLC
Chambersburg PA
CBHW041759040426
42447CB00001B/22